AMERICAN HEROES

RUBY BRIDGES

SCHOOL INTEGRATION HERO

by Becca Becker

pogo

Pogo Books, an imprint of Jump! Library by FlutterBee

Ideas for Parents and Teachers

Pogo Books let children practice reading informational text while introducing them to nonfiction features such as headings, labels, sidebars, maps, and diagrams, as well as a table of contents, glossary, and index.

Carefully leveled text with a strong photo match offers early fluent readers the support they need to succeed.

Before Reading

- "Walk" through the book and point out the various nonfiction features. Ask the student what purpose each feature serves.
- Look at the glossary together. Read and discuss the words.

During Reading

- Have the child read the book independently.
- Invite them to list questions that arise from reading.

After Reading

- Discuss the child's questions. Talk about how they might find answers to those questions.
- Prompt the child to think more. Ask: How can you make sure everyone is included at school?

Pogo Books are published by Jump!
3500 American Blvd W, Suite 150
Bloomington, MN 55431
www.jumplibrary.com

Jump! is a division of FlutterBee Education Group.

Library of Congress Cataloging-in-Publication Data

Names: Becker, Becca author
Title: Ruby Bridges: school integration hero
by Becca Becker.
Description: Bloomington, MN: Jump!, Inc., [2026]
Series: American heroes | Includes index.
Audience: Ages 7-10
Identifiers: LCCN 2025028208 (print)
LCCN 2025028209 (ebook)
ISBN 9798896623649 hardcover
ISBN 9798896623656 paperback
ISBN 9798896623663 ebook
Subjects: LCSH: Bridges, Ruby–Juvenile literature
African American girls–Louisiana–New Orleans–Biography–Juvenile literature | African Americans–Louisiana–New Orleans–Biography–Juvenile literature
School integration–Louisiana–New Orleans–Juvenile literature | William Frantz Elementary School (New Orleans, La.) –History–20th century–Juvenile literature
Teacher-student relationships–Louisiana–New Orleans–Juvenile literature | LCGFT: Biographies
Classification: LCC F379.N553 B42 2026 (print)
LCC F379.N553 (ebook)
DDC 379.2/63092 [B] –dc23/eng/20250909
LC record available at https://lccn.loc.gov/2025028208
LC ebook record available at https://lccn.loc.gov/2025028209

Editor: Katie Chanez
Designer: Molly Ballanger

Photo Credits: Bettmann/Getty, cover, 6-7 (bottom), 8-9, 10; Randy Duchaine/Alamy, 1; Diana Taliun/Adobe Stock, 3; GHI/Universal Images Group/Getty, 4; Paul Slade/Paris Match/Getty, 5; Heilman/Classicstock/Getty, 6-7 (top); Carlo Bollo/Alamy, 11; Lane Turner/The Boston Globe/Getty, 12-13; H. ARMSTRONG ROBERTS/ClassicStock/SuperStock, 14-15; Briannolan/Dreamstime, 16; William Morgan/Alamy, 17; Tina Fineberg/AP Images, 18-19; American Photo Archive/Alamy, 20-21; National Archives, 23.

Printed in the United States of America at
Corporate Graphics in North Mankato, Minnesota.

TABLE OF CONTENTS

CHAPTER 1

EARLY LIFE

Ruby Bridges was born on September 8, 1954. She lived in Tylertown, Mississippi. Her parents were **sharecroppers**. When Ruby was young, her family moved to New Orleans, Louisiana. Her parents wanted better jobs to make more money.

sharecroppers

Ruby made friends in kindergarten. All the students in her school were Black.

white school

Black school

For years, the southern United States was **segregated**. Laws said Black and white people could not be together. They had different schools, libraries, parks, and more. The places for white people were much nicer.

Many school buildings for Black students were falling apart. Students read from old books. Some Black schools didn't have books at all. These things made it harder for Black students to learn.

WHAT DO YOU THINK?

Do you think it is fair to separate people based on how they look? Why or why not?

In 1954, the **U.S. Supreme Court** said segregated schools were unfair. White schools had to **integrate**. They had to let Black students in. But many southern schools did not. **Activists** asked Black kids to go to white schools anyway. Ruby did.

TAKE A LOOK!

Which U.S. states would not integrate schools in 1958? Take a look.

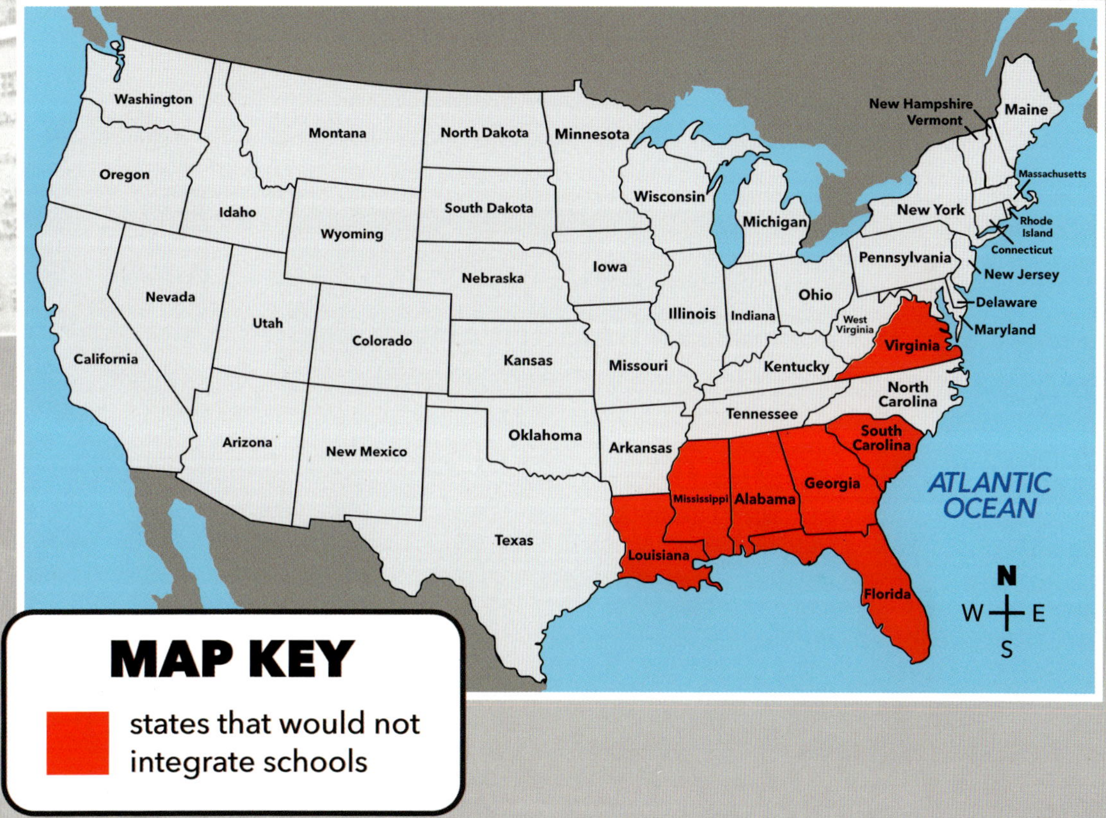

CHAPTER 2

GOING TO SCHOOL

On November 14, 1960, Ruby started first grade. She went to William Frantz Elementary School. It was a white school near Ruby's home. Ruby was the first Black student in the South to go to a white elementary school.

Many white people did not want Black children to go to the school. They stood outside. They yelled at Ruby as she walked by. They threw things. Law enforcement officers walked Ruby to and from school. They did this every day for one year. They kept her safe.

Barbara Henry

White parents took their kids out of the school. Ruby was the only student in her class. Only one teacher would teach Ruby. Her name was Barbara Henry.

Barbara made school fun. When people outside were loud and mean, Barbara and Ruby made music. Barbara made Ruby feel safe and loved. She was Ruby's only friend at school. They stayed friends even as Ruby grew up.

DID YOU KNOW?

White people were mad at Ruby's parents. Why? They did not want Ruby to go to William Frantz Elementary School. Ruby's parents were fired from their jobs. Grocery stores would not sell them food.

Write these names correctly
Dr.
Mr.
Mrs.
Miss

Eventually, white kids came back to the school. One boy told Ruby he couldn't play with her because she was Black. This hurt her feelings.

As years went on, things changed. More Black students went to white schools. Students of all **races** learned together. Ruby had paved the way for them.

WHAT DO YOU THINK?

Do you think Ruby's actions gave other Black students **courage** to go to a white school? Why or why not?

CHAPTER 3

MAKING A DIFFERENCE

Ruby grew up. She **graduated** from a high school with both Black and white students. In 2005, Hurricane Katrina hit New Orleans. It damaged homes. It damaged William Frantz Elementary School, too.

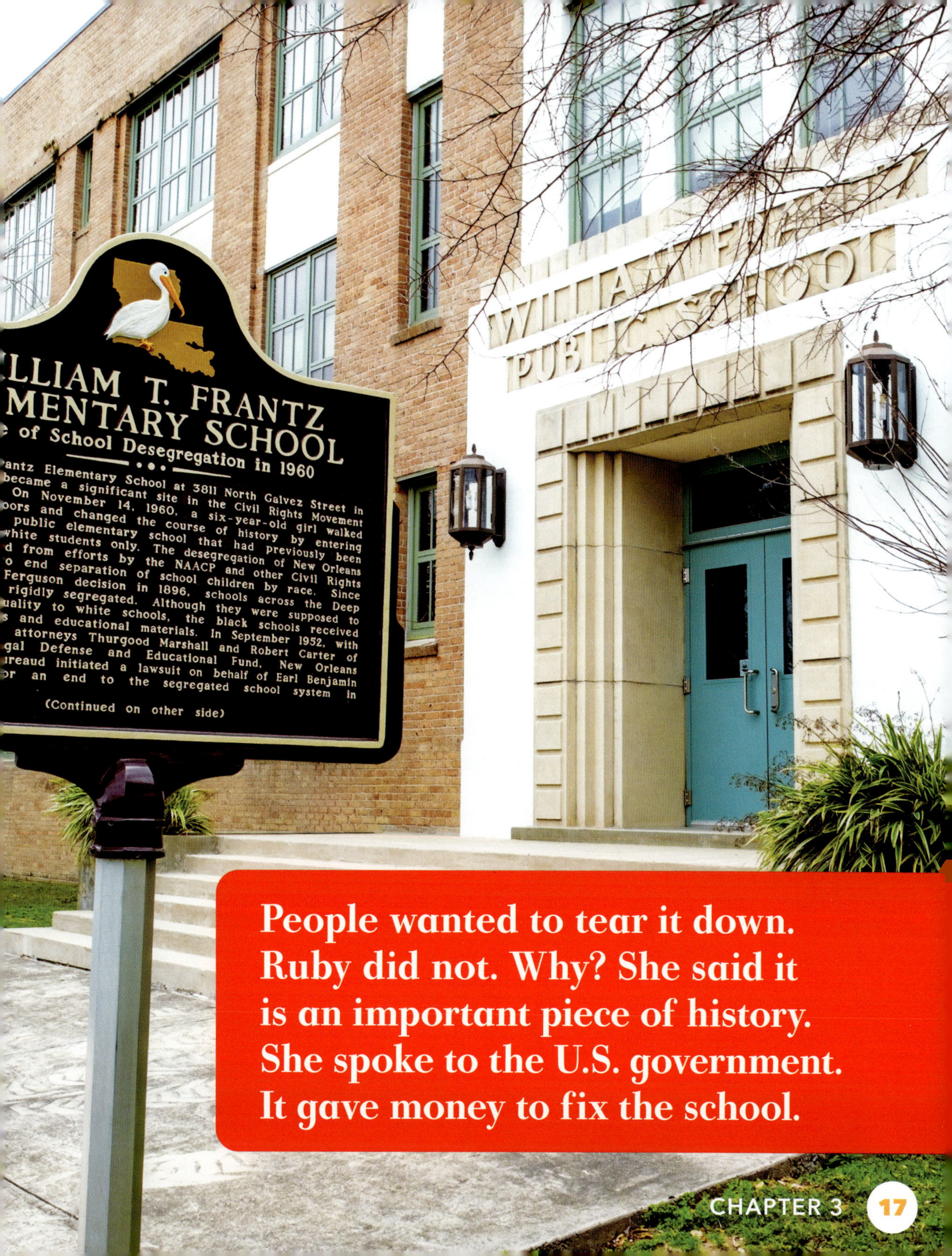

People wanted to tear it down. Ruby did not. Why? She said it is an important piece of history. She spoke to the U.S. government. It gave money to fix the school.

In 1999, Ruby started the Ruby Bridges **Foundation**. It works to end **racism**.

Today, Ruby is an activist. She visits schools. She reads to students. She shares her story with them. She tells them people can be friends no matter the color of their skin. Ruby wants everyone to be kind to one another.

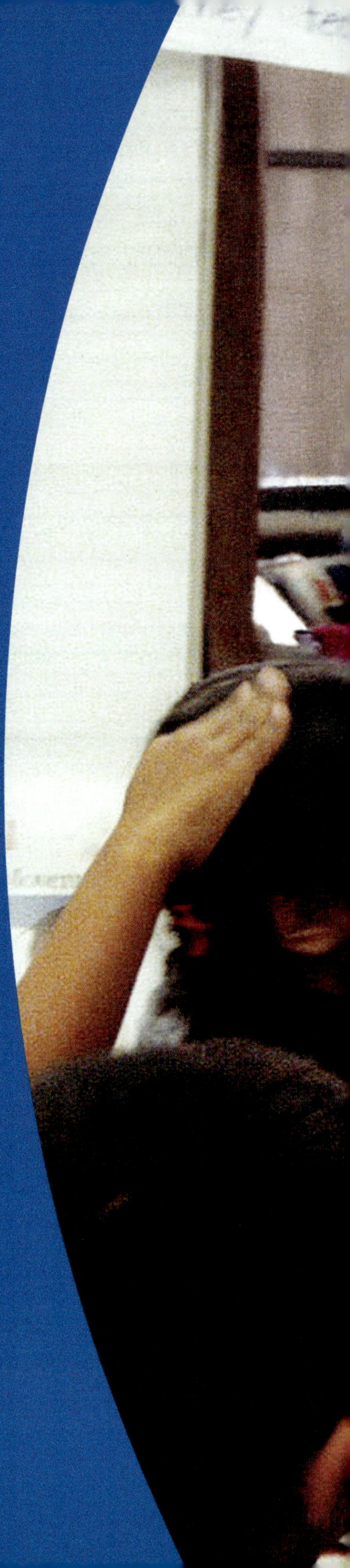

things

Ruby has written books for kids. She reminds them they can make a difference.

In 2011, Ruby met President Barack Obama. Obama was the first Black president. He told Ruby that if it were not for her, he wouldn't have been able to be president. Ruby has changed lives. She still tries to make the world a better place!

Barack Obama

QUICK FACTS & TOOLS

TIMELINE

What are big events in Ruby Bridges' life? Take a look!

SEPTEMBER 8, 1954
Ruby Bridges is born in Tylertown, Mississippi.

NOVEMBER 14, 1960
Ruby starts first grade at William Frantz Elementary School in New Orleans.

1998
Disney makes a movie about Ruby's experience going to a white school.

1999
Ruby starts the Ruby Bridges Foundation.

2003
Ruby writes a book about her life. It is called *Let's Read About Ruby Bridges*.

2005
Hurricane Katrina damages William Frantz Elementary School. Ruby saves it from being torn down.

2011
Ruby meets President Barack Obama.

2025
Ruby writes her seventh book. It is called *A Talk with My Teacher*.

GLOSSARY

activists: People who support a cause and believe in taking action to change things.

courage: The ability to do something that scares you.

foundation: An organization that gives money to worthy causes.

graduated: Finished school.

integrate: To include people of all races.

races: Groups that people are divided into based on their appearance.

racism: The idea that a particular race is better than others.

segregated: Separated or kept apart from the main group.

sharecroppers: People who farm land that another person owns.

U.S. Supreme Court: The highest U.S. court that upholds the U.S. Constitution and laws.

INDEX

TO LEARN MORE

Finding more information is as easy as 1, 2, 3.

1. Go to www.factsurfer.com
2. Enter "Ruby Bridges" into the search box.
3. Choose your book to see a list of websites.

FACT SURFER